KENTUCKY DERBY
GLASSES
PRICE GUIDE

FOURTH EDITION

A COMPREHENSIVE GUIDE TO
COLLECTING KENTUCKY DERBY
MINT JULEP GLASSES AND SHOT GLASSES

EP
ECLIPSE
PRESS

LEXINGTON, KENTUCKY

ISBN 978-1-58150-183-4

Library of Congress Control Number: 2007942969

Printed in the United States of America

Fourth Edition: 2008
First Edition: 1999

FiRST EdiTioN → ApriL 200

a division of
Blood-Horse Publications
PUBLISHERS SINCE 1916

Contents

Acknowledgments

The editor would like to thank the following for their assistance in compiling *Kentucky Derby Glasses Price Guide*:

John and Brenda Clark
Cindy Pierson Dulay
Ken Grayson
Dr. Merritt W. Marrs Jr.
Dwight D. New
Tom Sporney

Editor—Judy L. Marchman
Book Design—Brian Turner
Original Cover/Book Design—John D. Filer
Photography—Anne M. Eberhardt
2000 Derby glasses/shots, Breeders' Cup shots—Joy B. Gilbert
2005-2008 Derby glasses, 2005-2007 Derby shots, 2004-2007 Preakness, Belmont, and Breeders' Cup glasses and Breeders' Cup shots—Kirk Schlea

Kentucky Derby Julep and shot glasses through 2000 and Breeders' Cup shot glasses through 1999
courtesy of John and Brenda Clark

2001-2008 Kentucky Derby Julep glasses, 2001-2007 Derby shot glasses, 2001-2003 Preakness and Belmont glasses and 2001-2007 Breeders' Cup glasses and Breeders' Cup shot glasses courtesy of Dr. Merritt W. Marrs Jr.

Preakness, Belmont, Breeders' Cup glasses through 1999 and 2004-2007 Preakness and Belmont glasses courtesy of Ken Grayson

1938 Julep glass and Bakelites courtesy of Vic Regnaud

Photo of 1940 Dated glass courtesy of Philip Musial

Introduction

BY JUDY L. MARCHMAN / EDITOR

A rare, dated 1940 Derby glass for 15 bucks? You can't believe your eyes. It's Saturday morning, and you're at the local flea market. "Doesn't this person know what this is worth?" you think to yourself. It looks to be in good condition. You snatch it up. Score!

Most collectors of Kentucky Derby mint julep glasses are not going to be so fortunate as to find such an exquisite bargain. In fact, with souvenir glassware collecting on the rise in popularity, and with increasingly savvy sellers, it has become harder for collectors to know if they are getting a good price. For a beginning collector, just figuring out which glasses to look for and their relative value can be overwhelming.

1940 Dated glass is estimated to be worth $16,750.

The *Kentucky Derby Glasses Price Guide* provides new and established collectors with an average market value to go by when hunting for new additions to their collections. In this latest edition we have added photographs of several new Kentucky Derby glass variations, along with photographs of the regular official Derby glasses through 2008 and shot glasses through 2007. We also have updated the official Preakness and Belmont stakes drinking glasses, as well as the official Breeders' Cup glasses and shot glasses through 2007. Color images of these glasses are provided to help with identification. Tips on collecting Kentucky Derby glasses are provided in the following pages, and a quick reference list of current values is included at the back of this book.

Take time to examine the photos. Determine which glasses you want, what year you want to begin with, and how much you're willing to spend, then happy hunting!

Tips for Collecting Kentucky Derby Glasses

A few Kentucky Derby glasses picked up here and there have turned into a new obsession: collect all the glasses. But how to get started? Tom Sporney, a long-time Derby glass collector from Indiana, provided answers to some of the questions beginning collectors might ask. Another longtime collector, Vic Regnaud of Kentucky, offered some tips on looking at aluminum and Beetleware (Bakelite) tumblers.

What is the best strategy to take when starting a collection?

Conventional wisdom dictates that serious beginners should buy older glasses first, such as ones from the 1940s, '50s, and '60s. These are rarer and can go for much higher prices. Sporney offered some words of caution for beginners: purchase the older and less available glasses that you can afford within a somewhat flexible budget.

What does "mint condition" mean?

Mint condition indicates the glass is as close as possible to looking like it did straight from the factory, e.g., no scratches, chips, or fading.

What sort of things should I look for when examining glasses?

CHARACTERISTICS OF THE GLASS

- Roundness: variations in roundness greater than 1/32" to 1/16" range are easily visible.
- Top edge: minor enlargement of drinking lip at finish point acceptable as production standard, noticeable bulbous protrusion at finish point not desirable.
- Bubbles within the glass: small, incidental air bubble within glass acceptable as production standard. Multiple or large, visible air bubbles not desirable.

ALUMINUM CUPS

- Must be perfectly round with no major dings, dents, scratches, or acid stains.

BEETLEWARE (BAKELITES)

- Should be in excellent condition with good luster.
- All the printing in place on both decals.

PRINTING ON THE GLASS

- Completeness: no voids, uniformity of inking.
- Symmetry: centered indexing when different colors/screens are used.
- No fading or "loss of gloss": dishwashing, sunlight, etc.

GENERAL

- No physical scratches or gouges, in printing or on the glass.
- Distinguish between a "production error" and a "handling flaw."

What is meant by "mistakes" and "variations"?

It is really just a matter of nomenclature, just to distinguish one non-standard item from the "normal" one, and also to distinguish between production and flaw.

What kind of places should I frequent to look for glasses?

Don't hesitate to check anywhere and everywhere, even the obvious places. "Our best finds have been in the 'nah, can't be anything here' locations," said Sporney. "Cindy [Pierson Dulay, a fellow collector] and I split a set of four '74 Federals at the big monthly flea market in Atlanta when I walked over to unstack the dealer's display where he nested glasses."

Yard sales, flea markets, and off-the-road shops are still the best places to look for glasses, especially bargains.

What about the Internet?

The popular auction site, eBay, has become a key place to search for horse racing commemorative glassware. Bargains often can be found, especially for more recent glasses, but the rarer, older glasses still can generate intense bidding and high prices.

The best collector- and dealer-run sites include Tom Sporney and Cindy Pierson Dulay's The Equillector (www.about horseraces.com/equillector), a guide for collectors of horse racing memorabilia, and Joe Boone's The Derby Glass Page (derbyglass. com). A good index of dealer/collector sites and other equine collectibles sites can be found at Cindy Pierson Dulay's Horse-Races.net (www.horse-races.net).

Mint Julep

2 cups sugar
2 cups water
Crushed ice
Kentucky bourbon
Fresh mint

Boil sugar and water together for 5 minutes to make a syrup. Cool; place in covered container with 6 to 8 fresh mint sprigs. Refrigerate overnight.

Fill each julep glass with crushed ice; add 1 tablespoon of mint syrup and 2 ounces of Kentucky bourbon. Stir rapidly to frost outside of glass.

Garnish with fresh mint sprig. Enjoy!

(The Early Times recipe)

KENTUCKY DERBY
GLASSES
PRICE GUIDE

FOURTH EDITION

3,180

1938
$2,715

Some collectors do not consider this an "official" Derby glass. However, it is sought after as the starting point for many collections because it is dated and was used as a water glass at Churchill Downs on Derby Day.

1939
$5,370

6,100

570

1940
Aluminum
$380

These tumblers, including the French Lick version, are becoming difficult to find, especially in mint condition.

1940
Aluminum,
French Lick
$670

This version was produced by the French Lick Springs Hotel in Indiana.

900

1940

Undated glass
(shown)...**$16,250**
12,500
Dated glass
(see page 5)...**$16,750**
16,000
Both of these glasses
are considered rare and
are in great demand
with collectors.

1941-1944

Beetleware
$2,300/up
2,500/up

Also known as Bakelites, these tumblers
come in a variety of colors, including
red, blue, pink, brown, green, yellow,
and orange. They were produced during
World War II when glass and aluminum
were rationed.

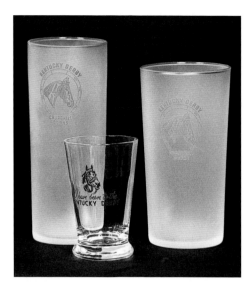

1945
Tall...$240 *390*
Short...$720 *1070*
Jigger ("Juice")...$735 *800*

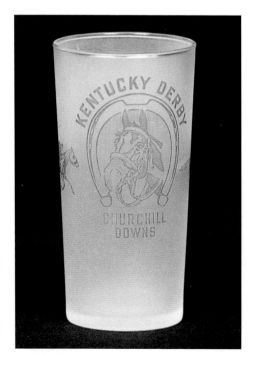

1948
Clear bottom...$125 *190*
Frosted bottom...$200 *220*

1949
$170
190
Variation with year
winner missing
$625
525

1950
$220
350

1951

$305

505

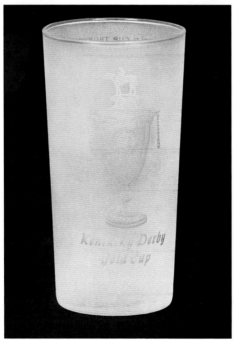

1952

$140

180

The "Gold Cup" Julep

1953

$80

130

This was the year that past winners started to be listed on a regular basis.

1954

$110

190

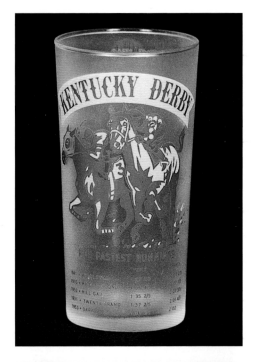

1955
$80 *125*

1956
2 stars, 3 tails...$170 *190*
2 stars, 2 tails...$120 *180*
1 star, 2 tails...$135 *190*
1 star, 3 tails...$390 *470*
"Headless jockey"...$1,500
(see page 44)

The color screening process went awry with this glass, causing several variations. The most commonly found ones are listed above.

GOT

1957
$65
/05

1958
Gold Bar (left)...$95
/85
Iron Liege...$110
205

The Iron Liege version was produced from overstocked 1957 glasses, restamped with the name of that year's winner.

1959
$45
65

1960
$40
70

1961

$55

100

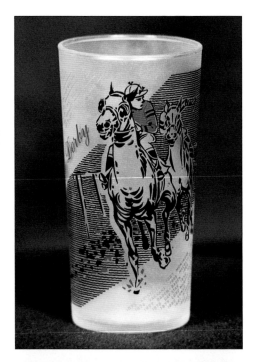

1962

$40

70

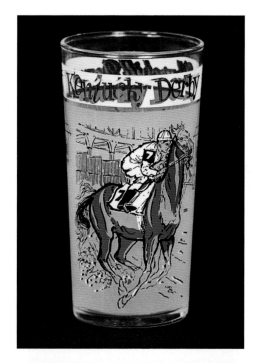

1963

$30

45

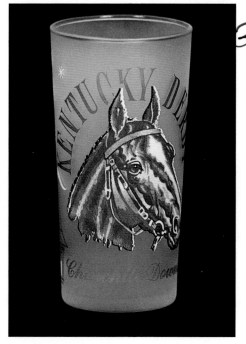

GOT

1964

$20

40

GOT

1965

$40

70

1966

$30

50

1967
$30
50

1968
$25
45

1969
$25
45
No past winners are
listed because of the
1968 disqualification
of Dancer's Image.

1970
$35
60
Type of glass used
breaks easily.

1971

$20

40

1972

$20

35

1973
$30 *50*
White background
(see page 45)...$130 *85*

1974
Canonero "Federal"
$120 *150*
Canonero II "Federal"
$130 *150*
Canonero "Libbey"
$8 *12*
Canonero II "Libbey"
$8 *13*

"Libbey" is Libbey Glass Co. and "Federal" is the Federal Glass Co. See the "Equillector" Web site (pg. 7) for more information about these glasses and their distinguishing marks.

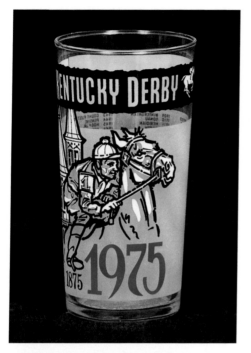

1975

$6

10

The plastic tumbler was
produced for the infield.

1976

Glass...$8 *13*

Plastic tumbler...$10 *16*

1977

$5

9

1978

$6

11

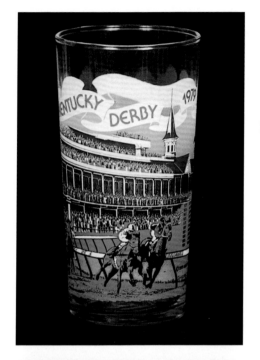

1979
$7

11

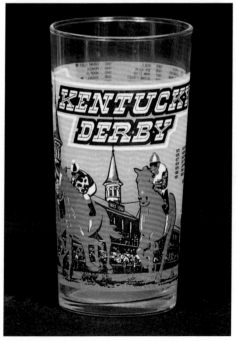

1980
$9 *17*

"Green screened" horse
(see page 45)...$2,000
1300
"Dark brown screened"
$100 *150*

1981
$6
12

1982
$6
12
"Red dot" missing
(see page 46)...**$340**
450

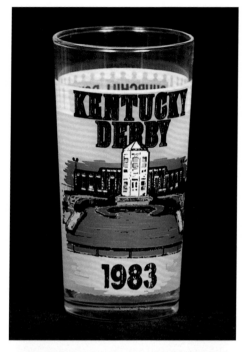

1983

$5 *8*

1984

$4 *8*

"Red dot" missing
(see page 46)...$250 *450*

1985

$5

9

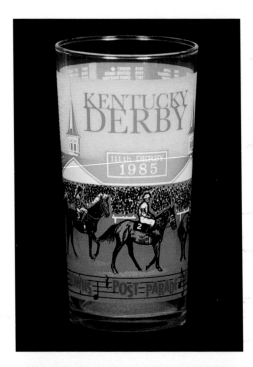

1986

1985 copyright...$10

1986 copyright...$5

11

"The Tiffany Glass"

1987
$4
8

1988
$4
8

1989

$4
8

1990

$3
7
"White" variation
(see page 46)...$25
100

1991
$3
7

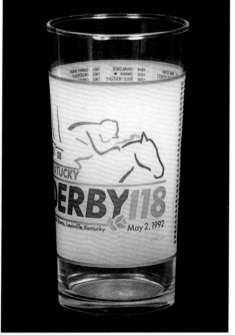

1992
$3
6

1993

$3

7

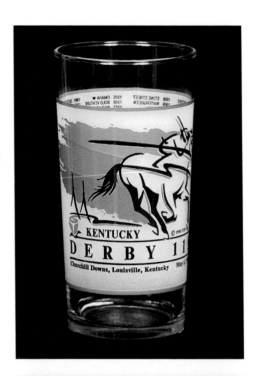

1994

$3 5

"White" variation
(see page 47)...**$20**

1995

$3

6

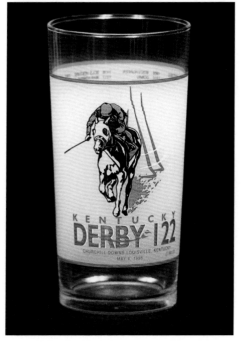

1996

$4

5

1997

$3

5

1998

$3

4

1999
$4
4

2000
$3 *4*
"Pink rose" variation
(see page 48)...**$85**

2001

$3

2002

$3

2003
$4

Triple Crown "mistake" glass
(see page 48)...**$4**

2004
$3

2005
$4

2006
$3
Secretariat's Derby
record variation
(see page 49)...$32

2007
$4

2008
$5

1946-1947

Leftover blanks from 1945. Some collectors do not consider these "official" glasses because they can be difficult to authenticate as actually being used at Churchill Downs.

No value available.

1956

The "Headless Jockey" variation that also has 1 star and 3 horse tails. Other variations include 2 stars, 3 tails; 2 stars, 2 tails; and 1 star, 2 tails.

See page 17 for prices.

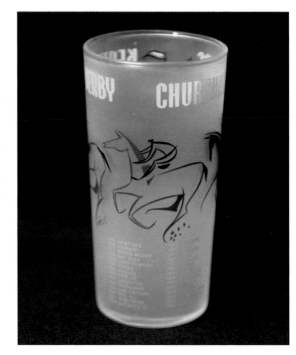

1973

A regular 1973 julep glass (left) and a "white" background variation.

See page 26 for prices.

1980

The rare "green screened" glass. Another variation is the "dark brown screened" glass.

See page 29 for prices.

1982, 1984

The "red dot" indicating a filly won the Derby was left off of Genuine Risk's name on some of the glasses in 1982 (left) and 1984.

See pages 30-31 for prices.

1990

Like 1973, this glass also has the white background variation (right).

See page 34 for prices.

1994

As with the 1973 and 1990 versions, this glass has a white background variation (right).

See page 36 for prices.

1997-2007

Ltd. Edition (1,000) 22k Gold Mint Julep Glass Series. Letters of authenticity are included.

1997...$130
1998...$60
1999...$60
2000-2007
(not shown)
$55-$60 each

2000

A regular 2000 julep glass (left) and the "pink rose" variation.

See page 39 for prices.

2003

This "mistake" glass has the Triple Crown symbol after Burgoo King's name instead of War Admiral's.

See page 41 for prices.

Signature Series

Begun in 1992, a limited edition series with the year's glass signed by the winning jockey.

1992...$175
1993...$125
1994/on...$50

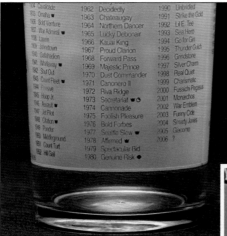

2006
$32

The regular 2006 julep glass with a stopwatch icon next to Secretariat's name indicating his Kentucky Derby and Churchill Downs record. Produced for Secretariat.com. 1,500 made.

2006
$2,000/up

Ltd. edition Woodford Reserve 24k-gold-plated julep cup with sterling silver sipping straw. Engraved with "Kentucky Derby 132" and "May 6, 2006." 50 made. Original cost $1,000. Proceeds benefited Thoroughbred Retirement Foundation.

2007
$25

Reproduction of 1957 Kentucky Derby glass. 3,000 made for Churchill Downs' "Turn-Back-the-Clock" promotion on June 10, 2007.

2007
$1,000

Ltd. edition Woodford Reserve 24k-gold-plated julep cup created by New England Sterling, the official Kentucky Derby trophy maker. 132 made. Each engraved with the name of a Kentucky Derby winner, from Aristides to Barbaro. Presented with sterling silver sipping straw. Proceeds benefited Thoroughbred Charities of America. The 1947 (Jet Pilot) cup is shown.

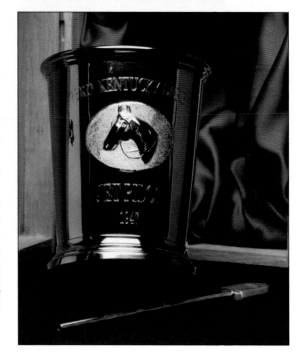

1987

3 oz. Jigger; clear with red and gold lettering $1,540
3 oz. Jigger; clear with black and gold lettering $325
1.5 oz. Shot; clear with red, black, and yellow lettering $175
1.5 oz. Shot; frosted with red, black, and yellow lettering $190

1988

3 oz. Jigger; clear with event logo $40
1.5 oz. Shot; clear with event logo $30
2 oz. Shot with handle; ceramic with event logo $150

1989

3 oz. Jigger; clear with event logo.................................. $30
3 oz. Jigger; clear w/event logo & Struck Equip. Co..... $400
1.5 oz. Shot; clear with event logo $20

1989

2 oz. Shot with handle;
ceramic with event logo
$150

1990

3 oz. Jigger; clear with event logo.............................. $340
1.5 oz. Shot; clear with event logo $20

1990

2 oz. Shot with handle;
ceramic with event logo
$110

1991

3 oz. Jigger; clear with event logo.................................$30
1.5 oz. Shot (Libbey); clear with event logo $30
1.5 oz. Shot (Korea); clear with event logo (not shown)...$50

1991

2 oz. Shot with handle;
ceramic with event logo
$150

1992

3 oz. Jigger; clear with event logo..$25
1.5 oz. Shot (Libbey); clear with event logo $20
1.5 oz. Shot (Korea); clear with event logo...........................$30
1.5 oz. Shot; black with gold logo $20

1993

Cordial with handle; clear with event logo/back copy $60
Cordial with handle; clear with event logo/no back copy.....$50
Cordial; clear with event logo/back copy $225
Cordial; clear with event logo/no back copy........................$50
Cordial with handle; clear with logo and gold lettering/no copy... $500

Note: This was the first year cordials were produced.

1993

1.5 oz. Shot (Libbey); clear with event logo **$25**
1.5 oz. Shot (Korea); clear with event logo (not shown)........ **$20**
1.5 oz. Shot; black with gold logo **$18**
1.5 oz. Shot; black with event logo...................................... **$17**
3 oz. Jigger; clear with event logo....................................... **$18**
1.5 oz. Shot; black with gold/solid screen logo................... **$250**

1994

Cordial; clear with event logo/no back copy **$10**
Cordial; clear with event logo/back copy **$14**
Cordial with handle; clear with event logo/no back copy..... **$12**
Cordial with handle; clear with event logo/back copy **$11**

1994

3.5 oz. Boreal with handle; clear with event logo $75
3 oz. Jigger; clear with event logo.. $14
1.5 oz. Shot; black with event logo...................................... $13
1.5 oz. Shot; clear with event logo $13

Note: This was the first year boreals were produced.

1995

3.5 oz. Boreal with handle; clear with event logo $8
3 oz. Jigger; clear with event logo.. $7
2 oz. Whiskey Shot; clear with gold and black lettering $12
1.5 oz. Shot; black with black Twin Spires in logo $8
1.5 oz. Shot (Hunter); clear with event logo $10
1.5 oz. Shot; black with white Twin Spires in logo.............. $100
1.5 oz. Shot (Libbey); clear with event logo $8

1995

Cordial with handle; clear with event logo/no back copy $7

Cordial; clear with event logo/back copy $8

Cordial with handle; clear with event logo/back copy $7

Cordial; clear with event logo/no back copy $8

1996

*3 oz. Boreal with handle; clear with etched event logo $50

3 oz. Boreal with handle; clear with event logo $8

Note: A number of "unauthorized" shots were produced for 1996. Production quantities of these could range anywhere between 72 and 500. These glasses are indicated with an asterisk(*).

1996

*Cordial with handle; clear with etched logo/no back copy $35
*Cordial; clear with etched logo/no back copy $35
Cordial; clear with event logo/back copy $8
Cordial with handle; clear with event logo/back copy $15
Cordial with handle; clear with event logo/no back copy $8
Cordial; clear with event logo/no back copy $15

1996

*1.5 oz. Shot; clear with etched event logo $40
*2 oz. Square Shot; clear with etched event logo $65
*1.5 oz. Paneled Shot; clear with etched event logo $60

1996

*1.5 oz. Shot; wine with event logo ....**Factory Sample**

No value available.

1996

1.5 oz. Shot; clear with event logo $6
*2 oz. Square Shot; clear with event logo $55
*1.5 oz. Paneled Shot; clear with event logo......................... $40
*2 oz. Flared Shooter; clear with event logo $35
3 oz. Jigger; clear with event logo... $6

1996

*1.5 oz. Shot; green with true etched event logo $60
1.5 oz. Shot; green with raised decal logo $10
      (Part of a set of three shots, including
      black and cobalt)...................... **$30 for set**
*1.5 oz. Shot; green with event logo $45

1996

*1.5 oz. Shot; black with etched event logo........................... $35
1.5 oz. Shot; black with event logo....................................... $14
1.5 oz. Shot; black with gold logo $10
      (Part of a set of three shots, including
      green and cobalt)...................... **$30 for set**

1996

1.5 oz. Shot; cobalt with gold logo $10
                       (Part of a set of three shots, including
                       black and green) .... **$30 for set**
*1.5 oz. Shot; cobalt with event logo $60
*1.5 oz. Shot; cobalt with etched event logo $45

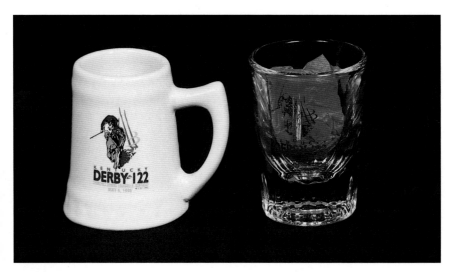

1996

*2 oz. Shot with handle; ceramic with event logo $75
2 oz. Whiskey Shot; clear with black and gold logo $11

1997

2 oz. Cordial; cobalt with gold event logo $10
1.5 oz. Shot; clear with black/gold graphics/lettering............. $6

1997

1.5 oz. Shots; wine, cobalt, green with gold event logo
　　　　　　　　　(sold as a set) $25
1.5 oz. Shot; black with gold event logo $10

1997

2 oz. Whiskey Shot; clear with gold event logo $6
2 oz. Whiskey Shot; clear with etched logo (Bacon's/McAlpin's
                          department store ltd. edition).............. $30
3 oz. Jigger; clear with gold event logo $10

1997

1.5 oz. Shot; ceramic with graffiti lettering $6
1.5 oz. Square Shot; clear with event logo $6
1.5 oz. Shot; clear with event logo $10
Cordial; clear with event logo/no back copy $10
1.5 oz. Shot; ceramic with event logo.................................... $6

1998

1.5 oz. Shots; black, green, cobalt with gold event logo
(sold as a set) $14
1.5 oz. Shot; black with event logo $10

1998

Large Shooter with handle; clear with event logo $13
Cordial; clear with event logo/no back copy $10
2 oz. Whiskey Shot; clear with gold event logo $7
2 oz. Whiskey Shot; clear with etched logo (Bacon's/McAlpin's
ltd. edition) $20

1998

1.5 oz. Shot; ceramic with event logo.....................................$10

2 oz. Square Shot; clear with event logo $10

3 oz. Jigger; clear with gold event logo $10

1.5 oz. Shot; clear with event logo $10

1.5 oz. Shot; clear with gold event logo — ltd. edition
(1/1,000); in Triple Crown set...............$25

1999

1.5 oz. Shots; cobalt, black, green with gold event logo
(sold as a set) $28

1999

1.5 oz. Shot; clear with event logo $9
2 oz. Flared Shooter; clear with event logo $9
Cordial; clear with event logo/no back copy $9
Cordial with handle; clear with event logo/no back copy $10
2 oz. Whiskey Shot; clear with event logo $8

1999
1.5 oz. Shot; clear with
gold event logo — ltd. edition
(1/1,000); in Triple Crown set
$35

1999

1.5 oz. Shot; clear with gold rim/wrap design with logo $10
2 oz. Whiskey Shot; clear with etched event logo (department
               store ltd. edition) (not shown) $12
1.5 oz. Stainless Steel Shot with event logo; ltd. edition (1/1,000) ... $22

2000

1.5 oz. Shots; cobalt, green, black with gold event logo (sold as a set) $20
1.5 oz. Shot; clear with gold rim/wrap design with logo $13
1.5 oz. Stainless Steel Shot with event logo; ltd. edition (1/1,000) $23
1.5 oz. Shot; frosted with event logo (Licensed Derby merchandiser
     All-Pro Championships' preview show exclusive) $55
1.5 oz. Shot; clear with event logo $9
Cordial; clear with event logo/no back copy $10
2 oz. Whiskey Shot; clear with event logo $7
2 oz. Flared Shooter; clear with event logo...$10
Cordial with handle; clear with event logo/no back copy $10

2000

3 oz. Jigger; clear with event logo...$17
2 oz. Whiskey Shot; clear with etched event logo (Dillard's department store
     limited edition)...$13
2 oz. Whiskey Shot; clear with gold event logo — ltd. edition (1/1,000);
     in Triple Crown set...$23

2001

1.5 oz. Shots; cobalt, black, green with gold event logo (sold as a set) $17
1.5 oz. Shot; clear with gold rim/red rose wrap design with logo... $10
1.5 oz. Stainless Steel Shot with event logo; ltd. edition (1/1,000) $18
1.5 oz. Shot; frosted with event logo (Licensed Derby merchandiser All-Pro Championships'
    preview show exclusive)... $40
1.5 oz. Shot; clear with event logo $9
Cordial; clear with event logo/no back copy $10
Cordial with handle; clear with event logo/no back copy $10
2 oz. Whiskey Shot; clear with event logo.. $8
2 oz. Flared Shooter; clear with event logo.. $10
2 oz. Whiskey Shot; clear with etched event logo (Dillard's ltd. edition) $25
1.5 oz. Shot; clear with gold event logo — ltd. edition (1/1,000); in Triple Crown set $20

2002

1.5 oz. Shots; black, green, cobalt with gold event logo (sold as a set) $20
1.5 oz. Shot; clear with gold rim/wrap design with logo $10
1.5 oz. Stainless Steel Shot with event logo; ltd. edition (1/1,000) $18
1.5 oz. Shot; clear with event logo $9
Cordial; clear with event logo/no back copy $10
Cordial with handle; clear with event logo/no back copy $10
1.5 oz. Shot; ceramic with event logo.. $10
2 oz. Whiskey Shot; clear with event logo.. $10
2 oz. Whiskey Shot; clear with etched event logo (Dillard's ltd. edition, 1/500).................................... $25
1.5 oz. Shot; clear with gold event logo — ltd. edition (1/1,000); in Triple Crown set $18
1.5 oz. Shot; frosted with gold event logo (Licensed Derby merchandiser All-Pro Championships'
    preview show exclusive) $40

2003

1.5 oz. Shots; black, green, cobalt with gold event logo (sold as a set)	$20
1.5 oz. Shot; clear with gold rim/wrap design with logo	$10
1.5 oz. Stainless Steel Shot with event logo; ltd. edition (1/1,000)	$16
1.5 oz. Shot; clear with event logo	$8
Cordial; clear with event logo/no back copy	$9
Cordial; frosted with event logo/no back copy	$8
1.5 oz. Shot; ceramic with event logo	$8
2 oz. Whiskey Shot; clear with event logo	$7
2 oz. Square Shot; clear with pewter logo	$9
2 oz. Whiskey Shot; clear with etched logo (Dillard's ltd. edition, 1/350)	$25
1.5 oz. Shot; frosted with gold event logo (Licensed Derby merchandiser All-Pro Championships' preview show exclusive)	$40

2004

1.5 oz. Shots; green, black, cobalt with gold event logo (sold as a set)	$15
1.5 oz. Shot; clear with gold rim/wrap design with logo	$10
1.5 oz. Stainless Steel Shot; ltd. edition (1/1,000)	$16
1.5 oz. Shot; clear with event logo	$7
Cordial; frosted with event logo/no back copy	$8
2 oz. Flared Shooter; clear with event logo	$8
1.5 oz. Shot; red ceramic with event logo	$8
2 oz. Whiskey Shot; clear with event logo	$5
2 oz. Square Shot; clear with pewter logo	$12
1.5 oz. Shot; frosted with gold event logo (Licensed Derby merchandiser All-Pro Championships' preview show exclusive)	$55

2005

Pictured is a sampling of the available shot glasses produced in 2005.

Most varieties
$8 to $20 each

1.5 oz. Stainless Steel Shot
$25

1.5 oz. Shot; with event logo and Woodford Reserve logo
$15

2006

Pictured is a sampling of the available shot glasses produced in 2006.

Most varieties
$8 to $20 each

1.5 oz. Stainless Steel Shots
$25 each

2007

Pictured is a sampling of the available shot glasses produced in 2007.

Most varieties
$8 to $20 each

1.5 oz. Stainless Steel Shot
$25

1973
$600

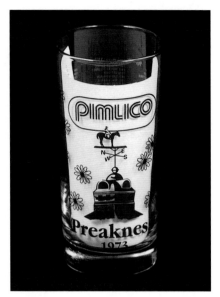

1998
$55

Silver replica of 1973
glass for Secretariat
25th Anniversary.

1974
$140

Shows the winners
of the Triple Crown.

1975
$40

1976
$35

1977
$35

1978
$60

1979
$30

1980
$35

1981
$30

1982
$30

1983
$30

1984
$25

1985
$20

1986
$20

1987
$17

1988
$17

1989
$20

1990
$14

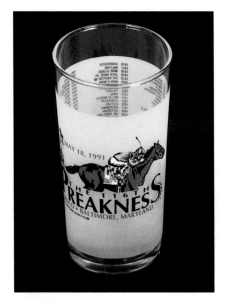

1991
$10

1992
$9

1993
$8

1994
$7

1995
$7

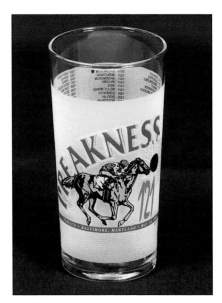

1996
$6

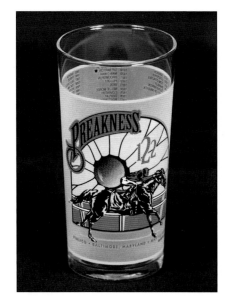

1997
$5

1997
$35

Ltd. Edition (1,000)
22k Gold Series.
Letter of Authenticity
included.

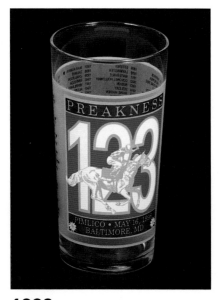

1998
$5

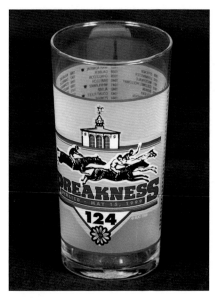

1998
$25

Ltd. Edition (1,000)
22k Gold Series.
Letter of Authenticity
included.

1999
$5

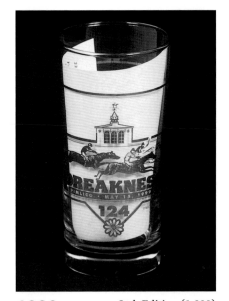

1999
$30

Ltd. Edition (1,000)
22k Gold Series.
Letter of Authenticity
included.

2000
$6

Ltd. Edition Gold,
not shown, $17

2001
$5

Ltd. Edition Gold,
not shown, $13

2002
$5

Ltd. Edition Gold,
not shown, $16

2003
$4

2004
$3

2005
$3

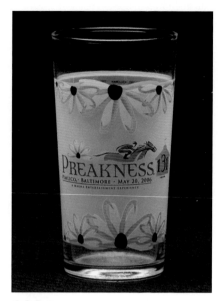

2006
$5

2007
$4

1976
$60

1977   This glass is rare.
$560

1978   Shows the winners
$90   of the Triple Crown.

1979
$40

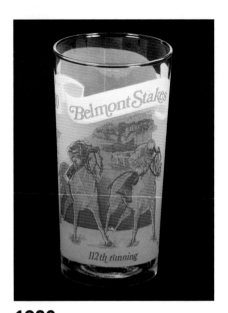

1980
$100

1981
$130

1982
$130

1983
$175

1984
$165

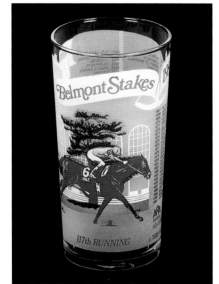

1985
$120

1986
$50

1987
$35

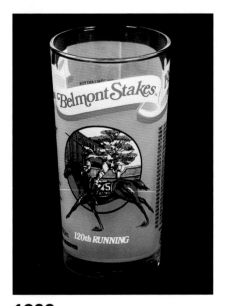

1988
$110

1989
$75

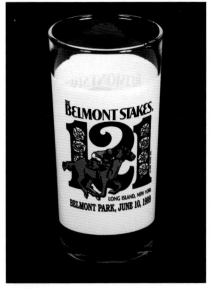

1989
$40

"Unofficial" glass

1990
$16

1991
$12

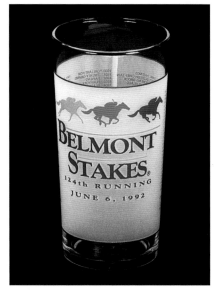

1992
$11

1993
$11

1994
$8

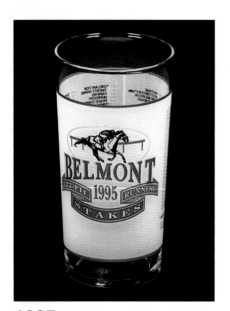

1995
$7

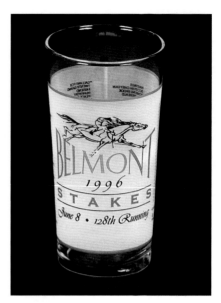

1996
$6

1997
$6

1997
$30

Ltd. Edition (1,000)
22k Gold Series.
Letter of Authenticity
included.

1998
$6

1998
$20

Ltd. Edition (1,000)
22k Gold Series.
Letter of Authenticity
included.

1998
$70

Secretariat
25th Anniversary glass. Letter
of Authenticity
included.

1999
$6

Ltd. Edition Gold,
not shown, $30

2000
$6

Ltd. Edition Gold,
not shown, $16

2001
$6

Ltd. Edition Gold,
not shown, $13

2002
$5

Ltd. Edition Gold,
not shown, $13

2003
$7

Ltd. Edition Gold,
not shown, $20

2004
$2

Ltd. Edition Gold,
not shown, $20

2005
$2

2006
$6

2007
$4

1985
$180

This glass is rare
and highly prized.

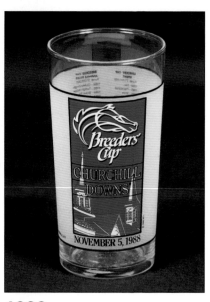

1988
$16

1989
$35

1990
$30

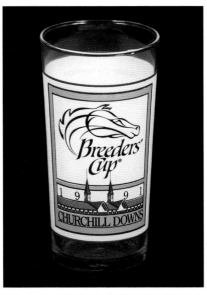

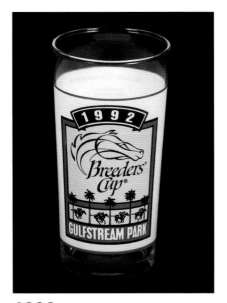

1991
$10

"Mistake" Glass lists French Glory as the winner of the 1990 Turf instead of In the Wings...$40

1992
$18

1993
$15

1993
$50

The Gold 10th Anniversary Glass. Letter of Authenticity included.

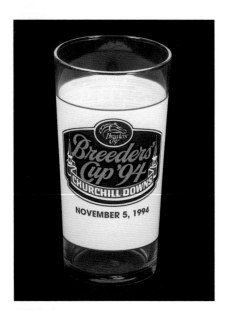

1994
$9

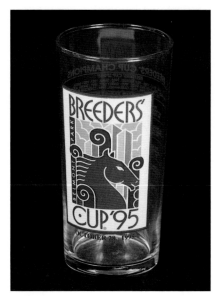

1995
$12

1996
$20

1997
$9

1998
$7

1998
$40

Gold 15th Anniversary Glass (1/1,000). Letter of Authenticity included.

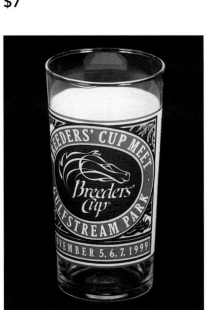

1999
$6

2000
$4

2000
$30

Silver Commemorative
Ltd. Edition
(1/1,000)

2001
$6

2002
$6

2003
$5

2003 Gold 20th Anniversary
$40 Glass (1/1,000)

2004 Frosted highball glass...$55
$6

2005
$7

2006
$4

2007
$6

(bottom row, from left)

1988 1.5 oz. Shot; clear/gold logo. No year listed on glass $20
1989 2 oz. Jigger; clear/white logo. No year listed. $45
   2 oz. Whiskey Shot; clear/gold logo. No year listed. $75
1990 2 oz. Whiskey Shot; clear/white logo. No year listed... $175

(second row, from left)

1991 1.5 oz. Shot; black/gold logo. No year listed. $50
1992 2 oz. Square Shot; clear/gold logo. No year listed. $50
1993 1.5 oz. Shot; black/gold logo (10th anniversary) $30
1994 2 oz. Square Shot; clear/gold with event logo. $25
1995 1.5 oz. Shot; clear/gold logo. $30

(third row, from left)

1996 2 oz. Whiskey Shot; clear/etched logo (only 1,000 made) $25
1997 2 oz. Square Shot; clear with event logo (only 1,000 made)................................ $45
   1.5 oz. Shot; ceramic with event logo (only 500 made) $75
   2 oz. Shooter; clear with event logo $20

(fourth row, from left)

1998 1.5 oz. Shot; frosted with event logo.. $20
   2 oz. Whiskey Shot; clear with event logo $20
1999 1.5 oz. Stainless Steel Shot (only 1,000 made) $16
   1.5 oz. Shot; wrap design (only 1,500 made)... $12

(top row, from left)

   1.5 oz. Shot; clear with event logo $8
   1.5 oz. Shot; ceramic with wrap design (numbered 1/1,999)................................ $12

2000

1.5 oz. Stainless Steel Shot; event logo $16
1.5 oz. Shot; ceramic in purple "Beetleware" design (only 500)... $50
2 oz. Whiskey Shot; clear with event logo $12
1.5 oz. Shot; clear with event logo $8

2001

1.5 oz. Stainless Steel Shot; event logo $19
2 oz. Whiskey Shot; clear with event logo $12
1.5 oz. Shot; clear with event logo $9

2002

1.5 oz. Stainless Steel Shot; event logo $18
2 oz. Whiskey Shot; clear with event logo............................. $12
1.5 oz. Shot; clear with event logo $9

2003

1.5 oz. Stainless Steel Shot; event logo $16
2 oz. Whiskey Shot; clear with event logo $10
1.5 oz. Shot; clear with event logo $7

(bottom row, from left)

2004 1.5 oz. Shot; clear with event logo $20
2 oz. Whiskey Shot; clear with event logo.. $40
1.5 oz. Stainless Steel Shot; event logo (not shown)............................ $40
(All varieties for 2004 are hard to find.)

2005 1.5 oz. Shot; clear with event logo $8
1.5 oz. Stainless Steel Shot; event logo... $20
2 oz. Whiskey Shot; clear with event logo (not shown)......................... $12

(top row, from left)

2006 1.5 oz. Shot; clear with event logo $8
1.5 oz. Stainless Steel Shot; event logo... $16
2 oz. Whiskey Shot; clear with event logo (not shown)......................... $10

2007 1.5 oz. Stainless Steel Shot; event logo... $16
1.5 oz. Shot; clear with event logo $7
2 oz. Whiskey Shot; clear with event logo (not shown)......................... $10

1996

1.5 oz. Shot; Cobalt/Etched Breeders' Cup logo

Factory Sample

1996

1.5 oz. Shot; Green/Etched Breeders' Cup logo with "Woodbine" lettering

Factory Sample

Year Unknown

These shots are factory samples, and thus no value is available. The tumbler has "November 21, 1987" and "Hollywood Park" etched on it. All are etched with the traditional Breeders' Cup logo.

Quick Reference Price List

To determine values for this price guide, several prominent collectors and/or dealers were polled as to what they consider a fair price for the Kentucky Derby, Preakness, Belmont, and Breeders' Cup glasses. The numbers were averaged to produce the values given below, which are intended to represent a "fair market value." The same method was used for determining the values on the Kentucky Derby and Breeders' Cup shot glasses. As with anything collectible, prices will fluctuate based on several factors, including buyer demand, location, and luck, and prices in the Louisville and Lexington, Ky., areas generally tend to be higher than in other parts of the country.

Kentucky Derby MINT JULEP GLASSES

Year	Value ($)	Year	Value ($)	Year	Value ($)
1938	$2,715	1964	$20	1986 (1986 copyright)	$5
1939	5,370	1965	40	1987	4
1940 (undated, glass)	16,250	1966	30	1988	4
1940 (dated, glass)	16,750	1967	30	1989	4
1940 (aluminum)	380	1968	25	1990	3
1940 (aluminum, French Lick)	670	1969	25	1990 (white background)	25
1941-44 (Beetleware)	2,300/up	1970	35	1991	3
1945 (tall)	240	1971	20	1992	3
1945 (short)	720	1972	20	1993	3
1948 (clear bottom)	125	1973	30	1994	3
1948 (frosted bottom)	200	1973 (white background)	130	1994 (white background)	20
1949	170	1974 (Canonero "Federal")	120	1995	3
1949 (year/winner missing)	625	1974 (Canonero II "Federal")	130	1996	4
1950	220	1974 (Canonero "Libbey")	8	1997	3
1951	305	1974 (Canonero II "Libbey")	8	1998	3
1952	140	1975	6	1999	4
1953	80	1976 (glass)	8	2000	3
1954	110	1976 (plastic tumbler)	10	2000 ("pink rose")	85
1955	80	1977	5	2001	3
1956 (2 stars, 3 tails)	170	1978	6	2002	3
1956 (2 stars, 2 tails)	120	1979	7	2003	4
1956 (1 star, 2 tails)	135	1980	9	2003 ("mistake")	4
1956 (1 star, 3 tails)	390	1980 (green horse)	2,000	2004	3
1956 (headless jockey)	1,500	1980 (dark brown)	100	2005	4
1957	65	1981	6	2006	3
1958 (Iron Liege)	110	1982	6	2006 (Secretariat track record)	32
1958 (gold bar)	95	1982 (red dot missing)	340	2006 (gold-plated)	2,000/up
1959	45	1983	5	2007	4
1960	40	1984	4	2007 (1957 reproduction)	25
1961	55	1984 (red dot missing)	250	2007 (gold-plated)	1,000
1962	40	1985	5	2008	5
1963	30	1986 (1985 copyright)	10		

Kentucky Derby SHOT GLASSES (H-handle)

Year	Style	Color—Lettering	Value ($)	Year	Style	Color—Lettering	Value ($)
1945	4 oz. Jigger	Clear—Green	$735		1.5 oz. Shot	Clear—Multi-Color Logo	$20
1987	3 oz. Jigger	Clear—Red/Gold	1,540		2 oz. Ceramic (H)	White—Multi-Color Logo	110
	3 oz. Jigger	Clear—Black/Gold	325	1991	3 oz. Jigger	Clear—Multi-Color Logo	30
	1.5 oz. Shot	Clear—Red/Black/Yellow	175		1.5 oz. Shot (Libbey)	Clear—Multi-Color Logo	30
	1.5 oz. Shot	Frosted—Red/Black/Yellow	190		1.5 oz. Shot (Korea)	Clear—Multi-Color Logo	50
1988	3 oz. Jigger	Clear—Multi-Color Logo	40		2 oz. Ceramic (H)	White—Multi-Color Logo	150
	1.5 oz. Shot	Clear—Multi-Color Logo	30	1992	3 oz. Jigger	Clear—Multi-Color Logo	25
	2 oz. Ceramic (H)	White—Multi-Color Logo	150		1.5 oz. Shot (Libbey)	Clear—Multi-Color Logo	20
1989	3 oz. Jigger	Clear—Multi-Color Logo	30		1.5 oz. Shot (Korea)	Clear—Multi-Color Logo	30
	3 oz. Jigger	Clear—Struck Equip. Co	400		1.5 oz. Shot	Black—Gold Logo	20
	1.5 oz. Shot	Clear—Multi-Color Logo	20	1993	Cordial (H) w/copy	Clear—Multi-Color Logo	60
	2 oz. Ceramic (H)	White—Multi-Color Logo	150		Cordial (H) w/o copy	Clear—Multi-Color Logo	50
1990	3 oz. Jigger	Clear—Multi-Color Logo	340		Cordial with back copy	Clear—Multi-Color Logo	225

Kentucky Derby SHOT GLASSES Continued

Year	Style	Color—Lettering	Value ($)
	Cordial w/o copy	Clear—Multi-Color Logo	$50
	Cordial (H) w/o copy	Clear—Logo; Gold Type	500
	1.5 oz. Shot (Libbey)	Clear—Multi-Color Logo	25
	1.5 oz. Shot (Korea)	Clear—Multi-Color Logo	20
	1.5 oz. Shot	Black—Gold Logo	18
	1.5 oz. Shot	Black—Multi-Color Logo	17
	3 oz. Jigger	Clear—Multi-Color Logo	18
	1.5 oz. Shot	Black—Gold/Solid Screen	250
1994	Cordial w/o copy	Clear—Multi-Color Logo	10
	Cordial w/copy	Clear—Multi-Color Logo	14
	Cordial (H) w/o copy	Clear—Multi-Color Logo	12
	Cordial (H) w/copy	Clear—Multi-Color Logo	11
	3.5 oz. Boreal	Clear—Multi-Color Logo	75
	3 oz. Jigger	Clear—Multi-Color Logo	14
	1.5 oz. Shot	Black—Multi-Color Logo	13
	1.5 oz. Shot	Clear—Multi-Color Logo	13
1995	3.5 oz. Boreal	Clear—Multi-Color Logo	8
	3 oz. Jigger	Clear—Multi-Color Logo	7
	2 oz. Whiskey Shot	Clear—Black Horses/Gold Type	12
	1.5 oz. Shot	Black—Black Twin Spires	8
	1.5 oz. Shot (Hunter)	Clear—Multi-Color Logo	10
	1.5 oz. Shot	Black—White Twin Spires	100
	1.5 oz. Shot (Libbey)	Clear—Multi-Color Logo	8
	Cordial (H) w/o copy	Clear—Multi-Color Logo	7
	Cordial w/copy	Clear—Multi-Color Logo	8
	Cordial (H) w/copy	Clear—Multi-Color Logo	7
	Cordial w/o copy	Clear—Multi-Color Logo	8
1996	3 oz. Boreal	Clear—Multi-Color Logo	8
	Cordial w/copy	Clear—Multi-Color Logo	8
	Cordial (H) w/copy	Clear—Multi-Color Logo	15
	Cordial (H) w/o copy	Clear—Multi-Color Logo	8
	Cordial w/o copy	Clear—Multi-Color Logo	15
	1.5 oz. Shot	Clear—Multi-Color Logo	6
	3 oz. Jigger	Clear—Multi-Color Logo	6
	Set of 3 1.5 oz. Shots	Black, Cobalt, Green—Gold Logo (Green—Raised Decal Logo)	30
	1.5 oz. Shot	Black—Multi-Color Logo	14
	2 oz. Whiskey Shot	Clear—Gold Logo	11

("Unauthorized" shots—all considered rare)

Year	Style	Color—Lettering	Value ($)
	3 oz. Boreal	Clear—Etched Logo	50
	Cordial (H) w/o copy	Clear—Etched Logo	35
	Cordial w/o copy	Clear—Etched Logo	35
	1.5 oz. Shot	Clear—Etched Logo	40
	2 oz. Square Shot	Clear—Etched Logo	65
	1.5 oz. Paneled Shot	Clear—Etched Logo	60
	1.5 oz. Shot	Wine—Multi-Color Logo	sample
	2 oz. Square Shot	Clear—Multi-Color Logo	55
	1.5 oz. Paneled Shot	Clear—Multi-Color Logo	40
	2 oz. Flared Shooter	Clear—Multi-Color Logo	35
	1.5 oz. Shot	Green—Etched Logo	60
	1.5 oz. Shot	Green—Multi-Color Logo	45
	1.5 oz. Shot	Black—Etched Logo	35
	1.5 oz. Shot	Cobalt—Multi-Color Logo	60

Year	Style	Color—Lettering	Value ($)
	1.5 oz. Shot	Cobalt—Etched Logo	$45
	2 oz. Ceramic (H)	White—Multi-Color Logo	75
1997	2 oz. Cordial	Cobalt—Gold Logo	10
	1.5 oz. Shot	Clear—Black/Gold Type	6
	Set of 3 1.5 oz. Shots	Wine, Green, Cobalt—Gold	25
	1.5 oz. Shot	Black—Gold Logo	10
	2 oz. Whiskey Shot	Clear—Gold Logo	6
	2 oz. Whiskey Shot	Clear—Etched Logo (Bacon's/McAlpin's Ltd. Ed.)	30
	3 oz. Jigger	Clear—Gold Logo	10
	1.5 oz. Ceramic Shot	White—Graffiti Design	6
	1.5 oz. Square Shot	Clear—Multi-Color Logo	6
	1.5 oz. Shot	Clear—Multi-Color Logo	10
	Cordial w/o copy	Clear—Multi-Color Logo	10
	1.5 oz. Ceramic Shot	White—Multi-Color Logo	6
1998	Set of 3 1.5 oz. Shots	Green, Cobalt, Black—Gold	14
	1.5 oz. Shot	Black—Multi-Color Logo	10
	Lg. Shooter	Clear—Multi-Color Logo	13
	Cordial w/o copy	Clear—Multi-Color Logo	10
	2 oz. Whiskey Shot	Clear—Gold Logo	7
	2 oz. Whiskey Shot	Clear—Etched Logo (Bacon's/McAlpin's Ltd. Ed.)	20
	1.5 oz. Ceramic Shot	White—Multi-Color Logo	10
	2 oz. Square Shot	Clear—Multi-Color Logo	10
	3 oz. Jigger	Clear—Gold Logo	10
	1.5 oz. Shot	Clear—Multi-Color Logo	10
	1.5 oz. Shot	Clear—Gold Logo (Ltd. Ed., 1/1,000; Part of Triple Crown set)	25
1999	Set of 3 1.5 oz. Shots	Green, Cobalt, Black—Gold	28
	1.5 oz. Shot	Clear—Multi-Color Logo	9
	2 oz. Flared Shooter	Clear—Multi-Color Logo	9
	Cordial w/o copy	Clear—Multi-Color Logo	9
	Cordial (H) w/o copy	Clear—Multi-Color Logo	10
	2 oz. Whiskey Shot	Clear—Multi-Color Logo	8
	1.5 oz. Shot	Clear—Gold Logo (Ltd. Ed., 1/1,000; Part of Triple Crown set)	35
	1.5 oz. Shot	Clear—Checkerboard Wrap	10
	1.5 oz. Stainless Steel Shot (Ltd. Edition, 1/1,000)		22
	2 oz. Whiskey Shot	Clear—Etched Logo (Bacon's/McAlpin's Ltd. Ed.)	12
2000	Set of 3 1.5 oz. Shots	Green, Cobalt, Black—Gold	20
	1.5 oz. Shot	Clear—Gold Rim/Wrap Design	13
	1.5 oz. Stainless Steel Shot (Ltd. Edition, 1/1,000)		23
	1.5 oz. Shot	Clear—Multi-Color Logo	9
	1.5 oz. Shot	Frosted—All Pro Premiere Ltd. Ed.	55
	Cordial w/o copy	Clear—Multi-Color Logo	10
	2 oz. Whiskey Shot	Clear—Multi-Color Logo	7
	2 oz. Flared Shooter	Clear—Multi-Color Logo	10
	Cordial (H) w/o copy	Clear—Multi-Color Logo	10
	3 oz. Jigger	Clear—Multi-Color Logo	17
	2 oz. Whiskey Shot	Clear—Etched Logo (Dillard's Ltd. Ed.)	13

Kentucky Derby SHOT GLASSES Continued

Year	Style	Color—Lettering	Value ($)
	1.5 oz. Shot	Clear—Gold Logo (Ltd. Ed., 1/1,000; Part of Triple Crown set)	.$23
2001	Set of 3 1.5 oz. Shots	Green, Cobalt, Black—Gold	...17
	1.5 oz. Shot	Clear—Red Rose Wrap Design	10
	1.5 oz. Stainless Steel Shot (Ltd. Edition, 1/1,000)		18
	1.5 oz. Shot	Frosted—All Pro Premiere Ltd. Ed. (1/576)	40
	1.5 oz. Shot	Clear—Multi-Color Logo	9
	Cordial w/o copy	Clear—Multi-Color Logo	10
	Cordial (H) w/o copy	Clear—Multi-Color Logo	10
	2 oz. Whiskey Shot	Clear—Multi-Color Logo	8
	2 oz. Flared Shooter	Clear—Multi-Color Logo	10
	2 oz. Whiskey Shot	Clear—Etched Logo (Dillard's Ltd. Ed.)	25
	1.5 oz. Shot	Clear—Gold Logo (Ltd. Ed., 1/1,000; Part of Triple Crown set)	..20
2002	Set of 3 1.5 oz. Shots	Green, Cobalt, Black—Gold	...20
	1.5 oz. Shot	Clear—Gold Rim/Wrap Design	10
	1.5 oz. Stainless Steel Shot (Ltd. Edition, 1/1,000)		18
	1.5 oz. Shot	Clear—Multi-Color Logo	9
	Cordial w/o copy	Clear—Multi-Color Logo	10
	Cordial (H) w/o copy	Clear—Multi-Color Logo	10
	1.5 oz. Ceramic Shot	White—Multi-Color Logo	10
	2 oz. Whiskey Shot	Clear—Multi-Color Logo	10
	2 oz. Whiskey Shot	Clear—Etched Logo (Dillard's Ltd. Ed.)	25
	1.5 oz. Shot	Clear—Gold Logo (Ltd. Ed., 1/1,000; Part of Triple Crown set)	...18
	1.5 oz. Shot	Frosted—All Pro Premiere Ltd. Ed. (1/576)	40
2003	Set of 3 1.5 oz. Shots	Green, Cobalt, Black—Gold	...20

Year	Style	Color—Lettering	Value ($)
	1.5 oz. Shot	Clear—Gold Rim, Wrap Design	.$10
	1.5 oz. Stainless Steel Shot (Ltd. Edition, 1/1,000)		16
	1.5 oz. Shot	Clear—Multi-Color Logo	8
	Cordial w/o copy	Clear—Multi-Color Logo	9
	Cordial w/o copy	Frosted—Multi-Color Logo	8
	1.5 oz. Ceramic Shot	White—Multi-Color Logo.	8
	2 oz. Whiskey Shot	Clear—Multi-Color Logo	7
	2 oz. Square Shot	Clear—Pewter Logo.	9
	2 oz. Whiskey Shot	Clear—Etched Logo (Dillard's Ltd. Ed.)	25
	1.5 oz. Shot	Frosted—All Pro Premiere Ltd. Ed. (1/576)	40
2004	Set of 3 1.5 oz. Shots	Green, Cobalt, Black—Gold	...15
	1.5 oz. Shot	Clear—Gold Rim, Wrap Design	10
	1.5 oz. Stainless Steel Shot (Ltd. Edition, 1/1,000)		16
	1.5 oz. Shot	Clear—Multi-Color Logo	7
	Cordial w/o copy	Frosted—Multi-Color Logo	8
	2 oz. Flared Shooter	Clear—Multi-Color Logo	8
	1.5 oz. Ceramic Shot	Red—Multi-Color Logo	8
	2 oz. Whiskey Shot	Clear—Multi-Color Logo	5
	2 oz. Square Shot	Clear—Pewter Logo.	12
	1.5 oz. Shot	Frosted—All Pro Premiere Ltd. Ed. (1/576)	55
2005	Most varieties		8–20 each
	1.5 oz. Stainless Steel Shot		25
	1.5 oz. Shot	Clear—Multi-Color Logo/ Woodford Reserve Logo	15
2006	Most varieties		8–20 each
	1.5 oz. Stainless Steel Shot		25
2007	Most varieties		8–20 each
	1.5 oz. Stainless Steel Shot		25

Preakness GLASSES

Year	Value ($)	Year	Value ($)
1973	.$600	1995	.$7
1974	.140	1996	.6
1975	.40	1997	.5
1976	.35	1997 (Gold Ltd. Ed.)	.35
1977	.35	1998	.5
1978	.60	1998 (Secretariat 25th Anniversary)	.55
1979	.30	1998 (Gold Ltd. Ed.)	.25
1980	.35	1999.	.5
1981	.30	1999 (Gold Ltd. Ed.)	.30
1982	.30	2000.	.6
1983	.30	2000 (Gold Ltd. Ed.)	.17
1984	.25	2001.	.5
1985	.20	2001 (Gold Ltd. Ed.)	.13
1986	.20	2002.	.5
1987	.17	2002 (Gold Ltd. Ed.)	.16
1988	.17	2003.	.4
1989	.20	2004.	.3
1990	.14	2005.	.3
1991	.10	2006.	.5
1992	.9	2007.	.4
1993	.8		
1994	.7		

Belmont GLASSES

Year	Value ($)	Year	Value ($)
1976	$60	1996	$6
1977	560	1997	6
1978	90	1997 (Gold Ltd. Ed.)	30
1979	40	1998	6
1980	100	1998 (Gold Ltd. Ed.)	20
1981	130	1998 (Secretariat 25th Anniversary)	70
1982	130	1999	6
1983	175	1999 (Gold Ltd. Ed.)	30
1984	165	2000	6
1985	120	2000 (Gold Ltd. Ed.)	16
1986	50	2001	6
1987	35	2001 (Gold Ltd. Ed.)	13
1988	110	2002	5
1989	75	2002 (Gold Ltd. Ed.)	13
1989 (unofficial)	40	2003	7
1990	16	2003 (Gold Ltd. Ed.)	20
1991	12	2004	2
1992	11	2004 (Gold Ltd. Ed.)	20
1993	11	2005	2
1994	8	2006	6
1995	7	2007	4

Breeders' Cup GLASSES

Year		Value ($)	Year		Value ($)
1985	(Aqueduct)	$180	1997	(Hollywood Park)	$9
1986	not issued		1998	(Churchill Downs)	7
1987	not issued		1998	(Gold 15th Anniversary)	40
1988	(Churchill Downs)	16	1999	(Gulfstream Park)	6
1989	(Gulfstream Park)	35	2000	(Churchill Downs)	4
1990	(Belmont Park)	30	2000	(Silver Commemorative)	30
1991	(Churchill Downs)	10	2001	(Belmont Park)	6
1991	(Churchill "Mistake")	40	2002	(Arlington Park)	6
1992	(Gulfstream Park)	18	2003	(Santa Anita)	5
1993	(Santa Anita)	15	2003	(Gold 20th Anniversary)	40
1993	(Gold 10th Anniversary)	50	2004	(Lone Star Park)	6
1994	(Churchill Downs)	9	2005	(Belmont Park)	7
1995	(Belmont Park)	12	2006	(Churchill Downs)	4
1996	(Woodbine)	20	2007	(Monmouth Park)	6

Breeders' Cup SHOT GLASSES

Year		Value ($)	Year		Value ($)
1988	1.5 oz. Shot	$20	2001	1.5 oz. Shot	$9
1989	2 oz. Jigger	45		1.5 oz. Stainless Steel Shot	19
	2 oz. Whiskey Shot	75		2 oz. Whiskey Shot	12
1990	2 oz. Whiskey Shot	175	2002	1.5 oz. Shot	9
1991	1.5 oz. Shot	50		1.5 oz. Stainless Steel Shot	18
1992	2 oz. Square Shot	50		2 oz. Whiskey Shot	12
1993	1.5 oz. Shot	30	2003	1.5 oz. Shot	7
1994	2 oz. Square Shot	25		1.5 oz. Stainless Steel Shot	16
1995	1.5 oz. Shot	30		2 oz. Whiskey Shot	10
1996	2 oz. Whiskey Shot	25	2004	1.5 oz. Shot	20
1997	2 oz. Square Shot	45		1.5 oz. Stainless Steel Shot	40
	1.5 oz. Ceramic Shot	75		2 oz. Whiskey Shot	40
	2 oz. Shooter	20	2005	1.5 oz. Shot	8
1998	1.5 oz. Shot	20		1.5 oz. Stainless Steel Shot	20
	2 oz. Whiskey Shot	20		2 oz. Whiskey Shot	12
1999	1.5 oz. Stainless Steel Shot	16	2006	1.5 oz. Shot	8
	1.5 oz. Wrap Design	12		1.5 oz. Stainless Steel Shot	16
	1.5 oz. Shot	8		2 oz. Whiskey Shot	10
	1.5 oz. Ceramic Wrap Design	12	2007	1.5 oz. Shot	7
2000	1.5 oz. Shot	8		1.5 oz. Stainless Steel Shot	16
	1.5 oz. Stainless Steel Shot	16		2 oz. Whiskey Shot	10
	2 oz. Whiskey Shot	12			
	1.5 oz. Ceramic Purple Shot	50			